T0414456

Blastoff! Beginners are developed by literacy experts and educators to meet the needs of early readers. These engaging informational texts support young children as they begin reading about their world. Through simple language and high frequency words paired with crisp, colorful photos, Blastoff! Beginners launch young readers into the universe of independent reading.

Sight Words in This Book

an	have	on	up
and	her	their	who
at	is	they	with
big	it	this	
down	look	time	
from	no	to	

This edition first published in 2022 by Bellwether Media, Inc.

No part of this publication may be reproduced in whole or in part without written permission of the publisher. For information regarding permission, write to Bellwether Media, Inc., Attention: Permissions Department, 6012 Blue Circle Drive, Minnetonka, MN 55343.

Library of Congress Cataloging-in-Publication Data

Names: McDonald, Amy, author.
Title: Owls / by Amy McDonald.
Description: Minneapolis, MN : Bellwether Media, 2022. | Series: Blastoff! Beginners. Animals in my yard | Includes bibliographical references and index. | Audience: Ages 4-7 | Audience: Grades K-1
Identifiers: LCCN 2021000776 | ISBN 9781644874745 (library binding) | ISBN 9781648343827 (ebook)
Subjects: LCSH: Owls--Juvenile literature.
Classification: LCC QL696.S8 M34 2022 | DDC 598.9/7--dc23
LC record available at https://lccn.loc.gov/2021000776

Text copyright © 2022 by Bellwether Media, Inc. BLASTOFF! BEGINNERS and associated logos are trademarks and/or registered trademarks of Bellwether Media, Inc.

Editor: Christina Leaf   Designer: Brittany McIntosh

Printed in the United States of America, North Mankato, MN.

Table of Contents

Owls!	4
Body Parts	6
The Lives of Owls	12
Owl Facts	22
Glossary	23
To Learn More	24
Index	24

Owls!

Hoo, hoo!
Who is this?
An owl!

Body Parts

Owls have wide wings. They have soft **feathers**.

feather

Owls have sharp **talons**. They grab food.

food

talons

Owls have big eyes. They turn their necks to look around.

The Lives of Owls

Most owls hunt at night. They spot **prey** from up high.

Owls fly
with no sound.
They sneak up
on prey.

prey

Owls **swoop** down. They grab mice and frogs.

mice

frogs

This owl brings food to her babies.

It is morning.
Time to
sleep, owls!

Owl Facts

Owl Body Parts

wings

feathers

talons

Owl Food

mice frogs birds

Glossary

feathers

the outer coverings of birds

prey

animals that are hunted

swoop

to dive down

talons

the claws of some birds

To Learn More

ON THE WEB

FACTSURFER

Factsurfer.com gives you a safe, fun way to find more information.

1. Go to www.factsurfer.com.

2. Enter "owls" into the search box and click 🔍.

3. Select your book cover to see a list of related content.

Index

babies, 18	morning, 20
eyes, 10	necks, 10
feathers, 6	night, 12
fly, 14	prey, 12, 14, 15
food, 8, 18	sleep, 20
frogs, 16, 17	sneak, 14
grab, 8, 16	swoop, 16
hunt, 12	talons, 8, 9
mice, 16, 17	wings, 6, 7

The images in this book are reproduced through the courtesy of: DnDavis, front cover; Michael Shake, p. 3; Chris Hill, p. 5; jps, p. 6; Richard Seeley, p. 7; Keith Bowser/ Alamy, p. 8; Eric Isselee, pp. 9, 22 (top); SunflowerMomma, p. 10; Marina Maytin Maduro, p. 11; Hana Duncova, p. 13; Design Pics Inc/ Alamy, p. 15; FotoRequest, p. 17 (top); Rudmer Zwerver, pp. 17 (bottom left), 23 (prey); Paul Reeves Photography, p. 17 (bottom right); Nature Picture Library/ Alamy, p. 19; Feng Yu, p. 21; Danita Delimont, p. 22 (mice); Todd Ryburn Photography/ Getty Images, p. 22 (frogs); ChrisCrafter, p. 22 (birds); Mathee Suwannarak, p. 23 (feathers); Jim Cumming, p. 23 (swoop); DeLoyd Huenink, p. 23 (talons).